The  Rumpy Pumpy

Quiz Book

Lynn!

To my neighbor, who I always ask for "push-push".

Yours,

Push - Push.

p.s. you want push-push?

RALPH STORER

The Rumpy Pumpy

Quiz Book

metro

Published by Metro Publishing Ltd,
3, Bramber Court, 2 Bramber Road,
London W14 9PB, England

www.blake.co.uk

First published in paperback in 2003

ISBN 1 84358 077 2

British Library Cataloguing-in-Publication Data:

A catalogue record for this book is available from the British Library.

Design by www.envyltd.co.uk

Printed in Great Britain by Bookmarque, Croydon

1 3 5 7 9 10 8 6 4 2

Papers used by Metro Publishing are natural, recyclable products made
from wood grown in sustainable forests. The manufacturing processes
conform to the environmental regulations of the country of origin.

To Those Who Have
Come Before

Contents

Foreplay

This is a quiz book for people who like sex.

That means you.

How do I know this? Because if you weren't interested in sex you wouldn't be reading this now. If you have picked up this book by mistake, put it down again immediately or be prepared to have your eyes opened and your mind expanded. Prepare yourself for the ultimate sex trivia challenge.

Sex is a topic of universal interest. Everybody knows something about it. Some think they know everything about it. Most would like to know more. Here's your chance to find out more and have fun at the same time. It's also a safe place to discover any gaps in your sexual knowledge without anyone else ever knowing – the ultimate in safe sex.

Some questions you'll find easy and satisfying; some are harder and more informative; some are curious and thought provoking. Some answers you'll know, some you won't. Some you'll think you know but don't. Some you'll think you don't know but you do.

There are yet more you may not wish to know.

Questions range from the detailed physiology of sex to the higher spiritual planes of sexuality, from universal truths to the outer limits of carnal knowledge, from useful techniques to curious customs. If you'd like to know whether cold water dampens ardour, or which exercises will increase pleasure, or when a Buddhist monk is permitted to ejaculate, or how a *guesquel* drives Patagonian women wild, or why the Victorians gave masturbation a bad press, or why people kiss under the mistletoe, or what Cleopatra used as a vibrator, or what is the sexual equivalent of origami, or ... this is the book for you.

There are those who would prefer to have

sex remain a mystery and, if there is one serious point to this slim volume (size isn't everything), it is to dispel such notions. It is time to consign to the dustbin of history the sex-negative attitude that has bedevilled Western society for hundreds if not thousands of years.

Sex won't make you fat or make you miserable or make you ill or damn you to everlasting hellfire. It is designed for pleasure. When evolution freed the human female from the oestrous cycle, enabling her to be sexually receptive at all times of the month, nature gave both sexes one of the most wondrous gifts in the animal kingdom, and a brain with which to appreciate it.

The female clitoris has no function but pleasure. The size of the male penis appears to have no function but the pleasure of the female. Sexual pleasure may originally have been intended as the motivating force for reproduction, but we have evolved beyond that. An adult human can have sex on his or her own, with a partner (of either sex), with or without emotional involvement, at any age, at any time and with a skeletal structure that allows a remarkable variety of positions.

So let this book be a celebration of sex in all its diversity. Let it encourage tolerance of the sexual behaviour of others, and let it reassure you that there is no sexual desire you can have that has not been had before at some time and in some place. There is nothing immoral about any pleasure to be obtained from any consensual sexual act of any kind. To suggest otherwise is a travesty against nature.

There are several ways to tackle the quizzes in this book. Like sex itself, you can enjoy it on your own or with others. It's as suitable for solitary quiz-surfing as it is for head-to-head combat with an opponent or between teams. Scoring is also a matter of personal choice. I suggest two points per correct answer, giving a possible total of twenty per quiz. This will enable you to award yourself one point for a nearly correct answer. Guesswork is encouraged – this is no place for bashfulness.

Some of the information presented herein may be open to minor argument (statistics, for instance, can vary from study to study), but I have done my best to ensure that all answers are correct. Please let me know if you think this is not the case.

Finally, sex is far too large and interesting a subject to do justice to it in a single volume. I am already collecting data for a second quiz book. Any help you can provide, dear reader, in the form of quiz topics or questions, will be gratefully received and acknowledged. Write to me at the publisher's address.

It remains for me to wish you good luck, and to hope that you get as much pleasure and satisfaction from this book as from the real thing (but if you do, then there's something you're not doing right).

Ralph Storer

Round the World Sex

Don't call the world dirty because you
have forgotten to clean your glasses.
PROVERB

1. According to World Health Organisation figures, approximately how many acts of sexual intercourse take place around the world each day?

    (a) 1 million?
    (b) 10 million?
    (c) 100 million?

2. Which European state has the world's lowest birth rate?

3. Many New Guinea tribes have traditionally been partial to semen. How did they take it?

    (a) As a toothpaste?
    (b) Baked in sago?
    (c) Stirred in coconut milk?

4. Which country is the nearest country to Britain in which you can join the mile-high club without leaving the ground? (1 mile = 5,280ft/1,610m)

    (a) Holland?
    (b) Belgium?
    (c) France?

5. The ancient Shinto ritual of *kagura* has been transformed in Japanese sex shows into the *tokudashi*, also known as 'The Open'. What does either involve?

6. In which country in 1987 was a star of porno films elected to the country's government on the platform: 'Down with the hypocrites who stop us having pleasure'?

    (a) Greece?
    (b) Italy?
    (c) Spain?

7. What is the Venus Temple in Amsterdam?

8. Which country has banned the import of Barbie dolls because they are 'a danger to sexual development'?

    (a) China?
    (b) Kuwait?
    (c) Morocco?

9. In one of the folk customs of the Austrian Tyrol, a man attempts to gain the affections of a woman by offering his handkerchief to her, for her to wipe her brow with during a dance. Where on his body has this handkerchief been held beforehand?

10. Where and when was the first sex shop opened?

(a) England in 1665?
(b) Australia in 1873?
(c) Germany in 1962?

2

Men's Bits

Nothing spoils a romance so much as
a sense of humour in the woman.

OSCAR WILDE

1. At approximately what age does the penis reach adult proportions?

>   (a) 13?
>   (b) 17?
>   (c) 21?

2. Is the penis more sensitive to touch before, during or after an erection?

3. What is the average speed at which semen ejaculates from the penis?

>   (a) 3 miles per hour?
>   (b) 14 miles per hour?
>   (c) 28 miles per hour?

4. Approximately how many spermatozoa are contained in a single ejaculation?

>   (a) 200 to 400?
>   (b) 200,000 to 400,000?
>   (c) 200,000,000 to 400,000,000?

5. What do the dartos and cremaster muscles do?

6. What percentage of men 'dress' to the left?

> (a) 50%?
> (b) 75%?
> (c) 99%?

7. Why does one testicle usually hang slightly lower than the other?

8. On an average night, how many erections does an average man have while asleep?

> (a) None?
> (b) 4 to 5?
> (c) 10 to 12?

9. What is the function of the prostate?

10. How many calories does the average ejaculate contain?

> (a) 30 calories?
> (b) 80 calories?
> (c) 130 calories?

3

Famous Lovers

Tell me whom you love,
and I will tell you what you are.
ARSÈNE HOUSSAYE

1. What did King Solomon make the Queen of Sheba do to her appearance before he would bed her?

2. Whose affairs with two Roman generals are celebrated in plays by Shakespeare and Shaw? Of legendary charm and sexual appetite, she is reputed to have serviced a hundred men in one night.

3. When British admiral Lord Horatio Nelson was killed at the Battle of Trafalgar in 1815, his last words were not for his estranged wife but for his beloved mistress. Name her.

4. Name the 12th-century lecturer and his student who became famous for their doomed love affair. After their secret marriage was discovered, he was castrated and became a monk while she became a nun. Their love letters made their story a lasting popular romantic tragedy.

5. Name the lover of Catherine II of Russia who became her most powerful minister before his death in 1791. A battleship was named after him, and a 1925 Eisenstein film

was named after the battleship.

6. According to legend, a queen and her champion became lovers, a sin that in Tennyson's *Idylls of the King* (1859–72) brought about the downfall of the kingdom. In Malory's *Le Morte d'Arthur* (*c*.1469), the queen renounces her lover after the king's death and becomes a nun. Name the lovers.

7. Name the two lovers who in classical Troy vowed fidelity by exchanging a sleeve and a glove. Their names are the title of a poem by Chaucer and a play by Shakespeare.

8. Which body parts did Lord Byron and Lady Carolyn Lamb exchange as a token of their love?

9. Name the tragic fictional lovers whose story first appeared in Masuccio Salernitano's *Novellino* in 1476. The hero poisons himself when he mistakenly thinks his lover is dead, and then she stabs herself when she finds his body.

10. Name the first of many lovers according to Hebrew legend.

4

True or False (1)

Truth is such a precious article
let us all economise in its use.
MARK TWAIN

Which of the following statements are true and which are false?

1. Man has the largest penis of all primates.

2. At the court of Henry VII of England, it was customary for ladies-in-waiting (royal attendants) to wear no underwear for the pleasure of the king.

3. Men snore more than women because they have more testosterone.

4. The German word for nipple is *Brustwarzen*, meaning 'breast wart'.

5. Queen Cleopatra of Egypt used a small box filled with bees as a vibrator.

6. Housewives have sex twice as often as working wives.

7. Rubbing nitroglycerine on to a penis makes it shrivel up.

8. Eskimo women have no periods during the Arctic winter.

9. For sexual stimulation, Louis XIV of France kept a rat in a specially designed codpiece. Tame rats were specifically bred for this purpose by the royal rat-keeper or *Gardien des Rats*.

10. A cold shower dampens sexual ardour.

5

Musical Sex

Musical notes and rhythms
were first acquired by the male or female
progenitors of mankind for the
sake of charming the opposite sex.

CHARLES DARWIN

1. Name the title of the Rolling Stones hit whose chorus had to be changed before the group was allowed to perform it on the 1967 *Ed Sullivan Show*.

2. Which 17-minute-long 1975 Donna Summer hit contains 22 orgasmic gasps?

3. Who reached Number 1 in both the UK and US charts in 1978 by wanting to know if you thought he was sexy?

4. Name the 1968 album whose cover features a naked John Lennon and Yoko Ono.

5. Which pop group named themselves after the amount of ejaculate per average male orgasm?

6. Who was arrested for allegedly showing his penis to the audience during a 1969 Miami concert? In 1970 he was found guilty of indecent exposure and profanity and sentenced to eight months' hard labour, but while appealing the sentence he died in a bathtub in Paris in 1971.

7. Name the 1984 spoof documentary about a rock group which features the immortal instrumental 'Lick My Love Pump'?

8. What kind of erotic therapy did Marvin Gaye recommend in his 1982 chart hit?

9. Who wanted your sex in the summer of 1987, thereby giving him a Top Ten hit in both the UK and US charts?

10. A track on the 1968 Beatles *White Album* is called 'Sexy ...' what?

6

Sexual Myths

The number of available orgasms
is fixed at birth and can be expended.
A young man should make love very seldom,
or he will have nothing left for middle age.

ERNEST HEMINGWAY

1. How did the English May Day custom of dancing round a maypole originate?

2. In ancient Greek and Roman times, which non-urogenital bodily function was recommended for contraception as a means of expelling sperm from the vagina?

3. Why did women in many ancient cultures lie in the rain?

> **(a) As a signal of sexual receptivity?**
> **(b) As a method of conception?**
> **(c) As a method of contraception?**

4. The gingerbread man was once a popular love potion. How was it used?

5. According to the influential teachings of Aristotle (384–322 BC), which governed scientific thought for two millennia, nature had three ways of generating new life. Sexual reproduction and asexual reproduction were two of these. What was the third?

6. Why did the Amazons, a legendary tribe of South American female warriors, break the arm or leg of captive men?

7. According to ancient Chinese teaching, what kind of offspring would result from the union of bisexual parents?

> (a) A bisexual child?
> (b) A hermaphrodite?
> (c) Twins – a boy and a girl?

8. Why did the Victorians object to masturbation?

9. Long before it was understood that conception requires both a man's sperm and a woman's egg, the ancient Greeks had two rival but equally mistaken theories about the part a woman's body plays in the process. Describe either of these theories.

10. Medieval Europeans lived in fear of the Incubus and the Succubus. Who or what were they?

(a) Evil spirits that molested people while asleep?

(a) Inquisition priests who checked on marital propriety?

(c) Satanic modes of transport that brought venereal disease?

7

Pot Pourri (1)

Sex is one of the nine reasons for reincarnation.
The other eight are unimportant.

HENRY MILLER

1. Nymphomania is an insatiable desire in women for sexual gratification. What is the male equivalent of nymphomania?

2. Among married couples, which of the following has the most sex?

(a) Couples aged 18–24?
(b) Couples aged 25–34?
(c) Couples aged 35–44?

3. 'Taint' is an American slang term for the perineum – the area between the scrotum/vagina and the anus. What is the origin of the term?

4. What is the difference between a bigynist and a bivirist?

5. What happens to the nose during sexual intercourse?

6. How did the custom of kissing under the mistletoe at Christmas originate?

7. Which food was invented to discourage masturbation?

    (a) Baked Beans?
    (b) Corn Flakes?
    (c) Muesli?

8. One of the two most popular shapes for female pubic hair sculpting is a triangle. What is the other?

9. Name the illiterate Siberian 'holy man' whose healing powers and doctrine of redemption through sexual release gained him popularity and political influence in imperial Russia. His penis, said to be 32.5cm (13in) long, was removed and preserved after his death.

10. Why is a kiss denoted by the letter X?

8

Fashionable Sex

A lady is one who never shows her
underwear unintentionally.

LILLIAN DAY

29

1. Name the whalebone framework worn by women in the late 19th century to expand the skirt and draw attention to the posterior.

2. The word 'brassière' was first used in English at the beginning of the 20th century to refer to a female undergarment. What does the word mean in French?

3. Who introduced chastity belts to Europe?

    (a) The Crusaders?
    (b) The Romans?
    (c) The Spanish conquistadors?

4. Name the item of apparel that was worn in Tudor times to highlight the bulge of the penis.

5. What was the 'kangaroo corset', invented by Frenchwoman Mme Gaches-Sarraute in 1900?

6. 'Petticoat discipline' was the name given to a method of keeping adolescent boys in check in public, used by mothers and governesses in Victorian Britain. How did it work?

7. When did Mary Quant invent the miniskirt?

> **(a) 1960?**
> **(b) 1965?**
> **(c) 1970?**

8. According to tradition, what item of a bride's apparel is a cure for impotence?

9. What is a merkin?

> **(a) A female pubic wig?**
> **(b) A penis extension?**
> **(c) An artificial beauty spot?**

10. What articles of clothing does Frederick's of Hollywood celebrate?

9

Sexy Words (1)

All words are pegs to hang ideas on.

H. W. BEECHER

What is the meaning of the following words?

1. BATHYKOLPIAN

 (a) Deep-bosomed.
 (b) Deep-buttocked.
 (c) Pertaining to a sexual practice
 involving Greek yoghurt.

2. URTICATION

 (a) Sexual application of raw onions.
 (b) Sexual application of whipped
 cream.
 (c) Sexual application of stinging
 nettles.

3. HODENSACK

 (a) A nightgown worn by medieval
 monks to discourage lustful thoughts.
 (b) The German word for scrotum.
 (c) A Celtic goblin who molested
 women at night.

4. MEABLE

(a) Victorian slang for a testicle.
(b) Marriageable.
(c) Easily penetrated.

5. BROCAGE

(a) A pimp's wages in Chaucerian times.
(b) A pubic wig in Elizabethan times.
(c) A type of bra in Victorian times.

6. TITILLAGNIA

(a) Sexual arousal from tickling.
(b) An obsession with breasts.
(c) A compulsion to tell dirty jokes.

7. BOGOMILES

(a) The Thracian god of carnal desire.
(b) Naked medieval Balkan Christian heretics who advocated free sex.
(c) A painful affliction obtained from certain sexual practices.

8. IATRONUDIA

(a) The state of having no pubic hair.
(b) Daydreaming about being naked.
(c) The desire of a woman to expose herself to a doctor.

9. MIN

(a) An Egyptian fertility god.
(b) Tudor slang for the female genitals.
(c) The ancient Chinese art of pubic hair sculpting.

10. TENTIGINOUS

(a) Well-endowed (of a male).
(b) Receptive (of a female).
(c) Lust-provoking.

Aphrodisiacs

Candy
Is dandy
But liquor
Is quicker

OGDEN NASH

1. The supposed aphrodisiac qualities of which eastern herb make it the most expensive in the world?

(a) Dong Quai?
(b) Ginseng?
(c) Mandrake?

2. Which dangerous irritant made from powdered beetles is perhaps the best known of all aphrodisiacs?

3. Some American Indian tribes used buffalo dung as an aphrodisiac. How?

4. Which shellfish did Casanova eat to improve his virility?

(a) Oyster (Ostrea)?
(b) Quahog (Venus mercenaria)?
(c) Whelk (Buccinidae)?

5. Which popular South American fruit was originally called a 'love apple' by the Spanish conquistadors who discovered it?

6. Name the glandular substance that is extracted from the abdomens of certain male deer to be used in perfumery. Ounce for ounce, it is the most expensive animal product in the world.

7. Which supposed aphrodisiac has caused one of the world's largest animals to be poached almost to extinction? To preserve remaining animals, the Zimbabwe government now surgically remove the much-prized part that the poachers are after.

    (a) Elephant tusk?
    (b) Hippopotamus testicle?
    (c) Rhinoceros horn?

8. Name the popular substance taken by many people unaware of its history as an aphrodisiac. It can be taken as a solid or a liquid and contains the chemicals phenylethylamine, a mood-altering chemical also associated with being in love, and theobromine (in Latin literally 'the food of the gods'). The Aztec King Montezuma II drank 50 cups a day to help him service his harem.

9. Name the expensive edible fungus, native to Europe, which was prized as an aphrodisiac as long as four thousand years ago in Babylon.

10. What do coffee and tobacco have in common?

Women's Bits

A curved line is the loveliest
distance between two points.
MAE WEST

1. What is the average length of an unstimulated vagina?

    (a) About 5–8cm (2–3in)?
    (b) About 8–10cm (3–4in)?
    (c) About 10–13cm (4–5in)?

2. What is the G spot and why is it so named?

3. Arrange the following phases of the monthly cycle in the order in which most women have the greatest sexual desire.

    (a) Before/at menstruation.
    (b) Around ovulation.
    (c) At/after menstruation
    (d) After menstruation.

4. 'Amatripsis' is a term used to describe a form of masturbation available only to women. Describe it.

5. Which of the following statements, if any, are true?

> (a) There is no such thing as female ejaculation.
> (b) The existence of female ejaculation has been scientifically proven.
> (c) Female ejaculation exists only in the sense that urine is sometimes ejaculated.

6. Do breasts contain muscles?

7. What is the average length of a clitoris?

> (a) 0.6cm (1/4in)?
> (b) 2.5cm (1in)?
> (c) 10cm (4in)?

8. According to the outmoded views of Freud, it is possible for a woman to be frigid even if she achieves orgasm. How come (or not!)?

THE RUMPY PUMPY QUIZ BOOK

9. What part of the external female sex organs is the fourchette?

10. Sex researchers Master and Johnson noted a 'tenting effect' during female orgasm. What were they describing?

(a) The ballooning of the inner vagina?
(b) The contraction of spinal muscles, causing arching of the back?
(c) The swelling of the breasts?

12

Historical Sex

History is merely gossip.

OSCAR WILDE

1. What does Valentine's Day commemorate?

2. According to figures collected by a Royal Commission, what percentage of Scottish brides were pregnant on their wedding day in the 1860s?

   (a) 10%?
   (b) 50%?
   (c) 90%?

3. In the 'cirque érotique' of 1930s Paris, naked women cycled round an indoor track. On what did spectators place bets?

4. In which decade were an ovum and a spermatozoon first observed?

   (a) 1450s?
   (b) 1670s?
   (c) 1860s?

5. One of the first recorded sex aids was made from wood or padded leather, and was known to the ancient Greeks as an *olisbos*. What was it?

6. Of the women questioned for the 1953 Kinsey Report, how many born before 1900 wore clothes while having sex?

      (a) One tenth?
      (b) One third?
      (c) Two thirds?

7. What was the 19th-century equivalent of the mile-high club, i.e. having sex on a plane?

8. When did Turkey outlaw polygamy?

      (a) 1928?
      (b) 1956?
      (c) Never?

9. The term 'libertine' today describes a morally dissolute person, but who were the first libertines?

10. In 1867 an article was published in the USA warning women against the dangers of sexual arousal when using a certain machine. Which machine?

(a) An adding machine?
(b) A sewing machine?
(c) A washing machine?

13

Pot Pourri (2)

Facts are apt to alarm us more than
the most dangerous principles.
JUNIUS

1. Medically, which organs determine whether a person is male or female?

2. In which year did *Playboy* magazine first appear?

  (a) 1946?
  (b) 1953?
  (c) 1960?

3. During his ground-breaking 1940s research on the physiology of female sexuality, what did Kinsey use to stimulate the sexual organs?

  (a) An artist's brush?
  (b) A cotton bud (UK) or Q tip (US)?
  (c) A gloved finger?

4. Which famous librettist/composer partnership wrote the comic opera *The Sod's Opera*, whose characters include Count Tostoff, the Brothers Bollox (a pair of hangers-on) and Scrotum (a wrinkled old retainer)?

5. At whom did the original Peeping Tom peep?

6. J. L. Milton's Victorian bestseller *Spermatorrhea* warned of the dangers of sperm loss through masturbation. Which of the following nocturnal anti-masturbation devices did it *not* recommend?

   (a) An erection restraint similar to a large bicycle clip?
   (b) Erection-triggered alarm bells?
   (c) A spiked penis cage?

7. Pheromones are sexual attractants secreted by the human body. They have no smell, so how are they detected?

8. In 1940, at the request of Miss Georgia Sothern, American humorist H. L. Mencken coined the term 'ecdysiast', based on the scientific term *ecdysis* (moulting), to give respectability to Miss Sothern's artistic profession. What was it?

9. What was the original meaning of the term 'virgin'?

10. Place the following activities in the order in which they are most likely to give you a heart attack.

(a) Heavy exertion such as jogging.
(b) Sexual intercourse.
(c) Waking up.

Censorship

Censorship ends in logical completeness
when nobody is allowed to read any
books except the books nobody can read.

GEORGE BERNARD SHAW

1. In which 1937 film was a scene censored in which men of restricted height build a bed for the star?

2. In 1967 the manager of a North Carolina cinema was arrested for showing the supposedly obscene Julie Andrews film *Hawaii*. Why was the film considered to be obscene?

3. Name the 1964 film starring Rod Steiger that was the first modern Hollywood feature to show a woman's naked breasts.

4. Which book broke century-old obscenity laws when publication was permitted following historic court cases in 1959 in the US and 1960 in the UK?

    (a) Fanny Hill?
    (b) Lady Chatterley's Lover?
    (c) Tropic of Cancer?

5. To which James Bond girl's name did American censors object, until the actress playing the part made the name respectable by being photographed with Prince Philip at the London première of the film?

6. When the BBC broadcast Arthur Ransome's famous children's book *Swallows and Amazons* in the 1960s, the name of one of the characters was changed to 'Kitty' to prevent embarrassment. What was her original name?

7. Which modern term for expurgation derives from the name of a Victorian editor whose ten-volume version of Shakespeare professed to remove 'everything that can raise a blush on the cheek of modesty'?

8. Under stringent rules introduced in the 1930s in Hollywood, known as 'The Hays Code', what was the maximum length of kiss allowed on screen?

(a) 3 seconds?
(b) 10 seconds?
(c) 20 seconds?

9. Which sexually controversial 1990 film about an American writer in 1930s Paris was the first to obtain the NC-17 rating from the Motion Picture Association of America? The rating was designed to separate a film of artistic merit from pornographic films, while at the same time prohibiting anyone under the age of 17 from seeing it.

10. How were pianos censored in Victorian times?

15

Marital Sex

Marriage is popular because it
combines the maximum of temptation
with the maximum of opportunity.
GEORGE BERNARD SHAW

1. What is the origin of the custom of carrying the bride over the threshold?

2. According to a 1951 study by C. S. Ford and F. A. Beach, how many of 185 societies around the world were monogamous?

> **(a) 16%?**
> **(b) 46%?**
> **(c) 76%?**

3. Any woman contemplating marriage should be *nubile*. The word today has connotations of sexual attractiveness, but what did it originally mean?

4. What was it that on his wedding night put Victorian art critic John Ruskin off sex for the rest of his life?

5. The largest mass wedding ever recorded took place in South Korea in 1988. How many couples were married?

> **(a) 1,357?**
> **(b) 6,156?**
> **(c) 10,000?**

6. The medieval custom of *droit du seigneur*, by which the king or local lord had the right to deflower a bride on her wedding night, originated in primitive times and was supposed to be for the benefit of the husband. How come?

7. What are the forms of marriage known as 'polyandry' and 'polygyny'?

8. Which is the only country in which same-sex marriage is legal?

(a) Denmark?
(b) Senegal?
(c) Thailand?

9. What is the origin of the custom of wedding guests kissing the bride?

10. What possessed Brahman Hindu men to marry a tree?

16

Like and Unlike (1)

Man has his will, but woman has her way.

OLIVER WENDELL HOLMES

What do the four items in each of the following questions have in common?

1. **Desert Shields   Mambas**
   Nite Glows   Ticklers

2. **Sarah Bernhardt   Guy de Maupassant**
   King Solomon   Elvis Presley
   of Israel

3. **Fratrilagnia   Patrilagnia**
   Sororilagnia   Thygatria

4. **The Fixing of a Nail   The Pair of Tongs**
   The Splitting of   The Swing
   a Bamboo

5. **Mahatma Gandhi   Sir Isaac Newton**
   Florence Nightingale St Swithin

Which of the four items in each of the following questions is different from the other three and why?

6. Cymbalism   Homosexuality
   Lesbianism   Sapphism

7. Cobblers   Marbles
   Niagaras   Orchestras

Clue: sexual slang

8. Deer   Elephant
   Mare   Tiger

Clue: types of vagina

9. Hexus   Nexus
   Plexus   Sexus

Clue: Miller's tales

10. Cinq à sept   Fling
    Flunch   Matinee

17

Sexual
Technique

Knowledge is a treasure,
but practice is the key to it.
THOMAS FULLER

1. The most common sexual position in modern Western society involves the man lying on top of the woman, face-to-face. Why is this position known as the 'missionary position'?

2. The Arabic term *kabazzah* describes a woman skilled in the ancient oriental sexual technique known in Sanskrit as *bhaga asana*, in which the man remains passive during sexual intercourse. What does the woman do?

3. What is the major benefit for the woman of *a posteriori* sexual intercourse, in which the penis enters the vagina from behind?

4. The *Kama Sutra* describes the 'butterfly flick' as a highly effective method of arousing a man. What is the butterfly flick?

5. Sex researchers Master and Johnson described four phases of sexual response: excitement, plateau, orgasm and resolution. They also noted a 'refractory period'. What is a refractory period?

6. What are 'Kegel exercises' and how can they improve sexual satisfaction?

7. Describe the sexual position that the *Kama Sutra* calls 'Reciprocal Sight of the Posteriors'.

8. The erogenous zones of the body are those parts that are especially sensitive to sexual stimulation. According to ancient Indian Tantric doctrine, there are three classes of erogenous zone or *marma*: primary, secondary and tertiary. Two of the three primary erogenous zones on both men and women are: (1) the genital organs; (2) the breasts and nipples. Name the third.

9. Describe the sexual technique known as *karezza* or *coitus sublimatus*, also known to (and forbidden by) the Catholic Church as *amplexus reservatus*.

10. In 1981 *Cosmopolitan* magazine conducted a survey among more than 100,000 women to discover what accompaniment or preliminary to sex they preferred. List the following replies in order of decreasing preference.

    (a) Alcohol.
    (b) Music.
    (c) Perfume or body odour.
    (d) Sex talk.

18

Royal Sex

I think the vulva of Her Most Holy Majesty
should be titillated before intercourse.
**ADVICE GIVEN TO MARIA THERESA
(1717–80), EMPRESS OF AUSTRIA,
ON HOW TO PROVIDE AN HEIR
TO THE THRONE.**

1. Who was the only gold medal winner not to be sex tested at the 1976 Montreal Olympic Games?

2. What punishment did Henry VIII mete out to any male staff who made his female staff pregnant?

(a) They had to go without beer for a month?
(b) They had to wear hair undergarments for the duration of the pregnancy?
(c) They were castrated?

3. Although male homosexuality was a criminal act in the United Kingdom until 1967, lesbianism was never illegal. Why not?

4. Champagne is traditionally drunk from wide, shallow glasses or coupes. On whose breasts were these supposedly modelled?

(a) Mme de Pompadour (1721–64), mistress of Louis XV of France?
(b) Marie Antoinette (1755–93), Queen of France and wife of Louis XVI?
(c) Marie Josephine (1763–1814), Empress of France and wife of Napoleon?

5. Why did Egyptian queens such as Cleopatra engage in incest with their brothers?

6. How many breasts did Ann Boleyn, Henry VIII's second wife, have?

(a) One?
(b) Three?
(c) Four?

7. Wigs were in vogue during the reign of King Charles II of England (1630–85). Of what were Charles' favourite wigs made?

8. How many of the first 15 Roman emperors were gay?

    (a) Four?
    (b) Nine?
    (c) Fourteen?

9. Who was pilloried by the British tabloid press in 1992 for podophilia?

10. How did Empress Wu Hu of the Chinese T'ang dynasty expect visiting officials to pay homage to her?

    (a) By kissing her naked breasts?
    (b) By performing cunnilingus on her?
    (c) By proffering their penis for her to hold?

Sexy Anagrams

Many a treasure besides Ali Baba's
is unlocked with a verbal key.
HENRY VAN DYKE

Can you find the words or phrases hidden in the following anagrams?

1. USE EXTRA HOLE

Clue: most people's inclination.
(1 word)

2. SURREAL EXECUTIONS

Clue: what most people indulge in.
(2 words)

3. I'M AS A MONSTROUS GLUE

Clue: what most people who indulge in 2 hope to achieve.
(2 words)

4. ATONAL JUICE

Clue: a possible end result of 2.
(1 word)

5. LARGE MOIST PLUMS

Clue: what some women have, while indulging in 2, that most men don't.
(2 words)

6. MORE SMOOCHY

Clue: what men possess that women don't.
(2 words)

7. MY! OH MAN! PANIC!

Clue: she wants sex!
(1 word)

8. SPORT TUITION

Clue: somebody always pays for it.
(1 word)

9. BUST ANIMATOR

Clue: manipulatory sex.
(1 word)

10. TRIPLE VOLCANIC PET

Clue: makes sex inconceivable.
(2 words)

20

Pot Pourri (3)

All debility of man must be attributed
to faulty exercise of the sexual act.

FROM THE TAOIST TEXT
THE PLAIN GIRL'S SU-NU CHING

1. The word 'erotic' derives from the Greek word *eros*. Who or what was Eros?

2. In the spring festival of the ancient fertility god Baal, what was the only way a woman could avoid having to offer herself sexually to male worshippers?

(a) By performing a sacred fertility dance naked?
(b) By having sex with a symbolic phallus?
(c) By shaving her head?

3. According to Freud, what is the male equivalent of 'penis envy' in girls?

4. What is an 'Arab strap' used for?

(a) To maintain an erection?
(b) To restrain an erection?
(c) To lubricate the vagina?

5. How is the penis formed during the female-to-male gender reassignment ('sex change') operation?

6. According to English folklore, what does a girl do with apple pips to determine which of several suitors truly loves her?

    (a) Bite them?
    (b) Plant them?
    (c) Throw them on the fire?

7. What and where is the Nobel Sperm Bank?

8. Which sexual behaviour was described by Kinsey in 1953 as 'physical contacts between males and females which do not involve a union of the genitalia ... (but) which involve a deliberate attempt to effect erotic arousal'?

    (a) Petting?
    (b) Kissing?
    (c) Playing footsie?

9. What is the origin of the superstition that a horseshoe nailed above a doorway brings luck?

10. More than 60% of women report having erotic fantasies during sexual intercourse. Arrange the following fantasies according to their frequency of occurrence.

(a) Satisfying more than one man.
(b) Being overpowered and forced to surrender.
(c) Acting as a prostitute.
(d) Being made love to by an imaginary lover.

21

Literary Sex

What is pornography to one man
is the laughter of genius to another.
D. H. LAWRENCE

1. Name John Cleland's 1750 book, perhaps the most famous erotic novel ever written, which was an abridgement of his earlier *Memoirs of a Woman of Pleasure*.

2. Name the celebrated 4th-century Hindu manual on love and sex, said to have been compiled by the Brahmin priest Vatsyayana.

3. Name the celebrated 16th-century Arabian book of erotic fantasies and sexual instruction written by the Tunisian Sheikh Umar ibn Muhammed al-Nefzawi.

4. Name the Victorian explorer and polymath who explored the sources of the Nile and was the first non-Muslim to visit Mecca (in disguise). He translated many erotic works into English, including the books in the previous two questions, thereby assuring their notoriety in the Western world.

5. Which diarist and novelist was commissioned by a wealthy patron in 1940s Paris to write erotica for a dollar a day. Collected and published in the 1970s in *Delta of Venus* and *Little Birds*, her stories have become classics of female erotica.

6. After writing the worthy *Robinson Crusoe*, Daniel Defoe turned his hand in 1722 to a bawdier novel whose titular heroine, among many other adventures, marries her brother and becomes a prostitute. Name the novel.

7. Name the Danish fairytale writer who was frightened of sex all his life. At the age of 62 he plucked up the courage to visit a Parisian brothel but made his escape before availing himself of its services.

8. To what did English humorist Edward Lear, whose 1846 *Book of Nonsense* popularised the limerick, attribute his epileptic fits?

9. The musical comedy *My Fair Lady* is based on a 1913 play by George Bernard Shaw. The hero, after whom the play is named, was a legendary Greek who developed agalmatophilia. Name the play.

10. Which respectable rector's daughter inadvertently wrote in a still-popular 1816 novel about a place where 'young ladies for enormous pay might be screwed out of health and into vanity'?

True or False (2)

When my love swears that she is made of truth,
I do believe her, though I know she lies.

WILLIAM SHAKESPEARE

Which of the following statements are true and which are false?

1. Tribesmen in northern Uganda can tie a knot in their penis.

2. Male and female embryos develop different reproductive organs from the time of fertilisation, depending on whether the ovum is fertilised by a male (Y chromosome) or female (X chromosome) sperm.

3. Empress Catherine II of Russia had her lovers sleep in the company of boars because the scent of boar's sweat was believed to increase sexual potency.

4. There is no correlation between the size of a woman's lips and the size of her genital labia.

5. New Guinea tribes tried to halt the spread of white man's venereal disease by holding orgies.

6. The Roman Emperor Tiberius trained young boys to swim after him in the pool and suck and nibble his genitals.

7. *Cassoulet* is the name given to a woman's sexual odour.

8. Man is the only animal that exhibits homosexual as well as heterosexual behaviour.

9. The word 'testicle' derives from the Latin word for witness, because it was the custom for a man in court to hold his testicles while swearing an oath, just as a Christian witness places a hand on a Bible.

10. Napoleon only attacked superior forces when he awoke with an erection, believing that it would make him victorious whatever the odds.

23

Animal Sex

The ability to make love frivolously
is the chief characteristic which distinguishes
human beings from the beasts.

HEYWOOD BROUN

1. Which mammal has the largest sperm?

   (a) A mouse?
   (b) A man?
   (c) An elephant?

2. The male kangaroo has a double-headed penis designed to fit the female's twin-horned vagina. What else is peculiar about the formation of the male kangaroo's penis and scrotum?

3. On what part of the body is the vagina of a female octopus?

4. How do male deer masturbate?

5. How do female threadworms, secure in their host vegetables, attract male threadworms for sex?

6. Name the creature whose male has the largest penis in the animal kingdom (3m/10ft long and 30cm/12in in diameter) and whose female has the longest clitoris tip (8cm/3¼in)

    (a) The elephant?
    (b) The giant squid?
    (c) The whale?

7. Of all the apes, only the female gibbon is monogamous. It has been suggested that this is because it is the only ape that has something in common with the human female. What?

8. What do female apes – apart from gibbons – have to gain from adultery?

9. The male elephant and male bat both possess a motile penis. What does this do?

10. Why does a female cat cry out when a tomcat withdraws after sexual intercourse?

24

Contraception

Contraceptives should be used
on every conceivable occasion.
SPIKE MILLIGAN

1. How were lemons once used as contraceptives?

2. With which of the following was the discovery of the contraceptive properties of intrauterine devices (IUDs) linked?

   (a) Camels?
   (b) Dildoes?
   (c) Drug smuggling?

3. Condoms were first widely used as contraceptives in the 18th century, but they had another use before then. What was their original purpose?

4. From which one of the following materials were 18th-century condoms *not* made?

   (a) Animal bladder?
   (b) Animal gut?
   (c) Animal intestine?
   (d) Fish skin?

5. Of which three words is 'Durex', a popular British condom, an acronym?

6. The rhythm method of contraception, in which sexual intercourse is restricted to the time of the month when a woman is least likely to conceive, is known as 'Vatican roulette' because it is the only contraceptive method approved by the Catholic Church. When was this approval given?

(a) 1290?
(b) 1660?
(c) 1930?

7. In ancient Egypt it came from a crocodile and in ancient Rome it came from a mouse. Which animal excretion was inserted into the vagina to prevent conception?

8. Until Christian missionaries reached the Solomon Islands in the 1930s, the idea of contraception was alien to the local Bellonese. Why?

(a) Large families were prized?
(b) They did not link conception with sexual intercourse?
(c) In a matriarchal society, pregnant women were viewed as highly

attractive and desirable, especially as their condition traditionally permitted them to take multiple sexual partners without fear of further, extra-marital, impregnation?

9. In which appropriately named French town was a contraceptive museum opened in 1994?

(a) Condom?
(b) La Pille?
(c) Le Cap?

10. What is the most effective method of contraception?

25

Unconventional Sex

There is no norm in sex.
Norm is the name of a guy
who lives in Brooklyn.
ALEX COMFORT

THE RUMPY PUMPY QUIZ BOOK

1. What can an autopederast do?

2. What did certain African tribeswomen do to obtain what was known as a Hottentot apron?

    (a) Plait fronds of grass into their pubic hair?
    (b) Stretch their labia minora?
    (c) Wear a belt of animal penis amulets?

3. Name the oral practice that, according to Kinsey, arouses 50% of sexual partners. The *Kama Sutra* lists eight different ways of doing it, including The Line of Jewels and The Broken Cloud, but it could be painful if done without care.

4. What was the painful manual practice at which women in Moorish bathhouses were so skilled that some men paid for their services to achieve orgasm?

(a) Removal of pubic hair by pulling it out in clusters?
(b) Scratching with specially manicured nails?
(c) Testicle kneading?

5. 'Axillism' is a form of safe sex that provides a tight fit and friction for the man but little sexual satisfaction for the woman. Where does an axillist put his penis?

6. Which sexual practice in Victorian Britain became known as 'le vice Anglaise' or 'the English vice'?

(a) Flagellation?
(b) Masturbation?
(c) Sodomy?

7. The term 'sadism' refers to the practice of obtaining sexual pleasure from inflicting pain on others. The term 'masochism' refers to the

practice of obtaining sexual pleasure from experiencing pain inflicted by others. Sadism is named after the Marquis de Sade, but where does masochism come from?

8. What kind of penile adornment is a Prince Albert, named after Queen Victoria's husband?

9. In French 'à cheval' means 'on horseback'. To which sexual practice did the term 'coitus à cheval' originally refer?

> **(a) Sexual intercourse in which one partner sits or kneels astride the other?**
> **(b) A sex game in which one partner acts as a horse and the other as a rider?**
> **(c) Sexual intercourse on a horse?**

10. Origami is the ancient Japanese art of paper folding, but what is its sexual equivalent – *tsutsumi*?

Pot Pourri (4)

It is one of the superstitions
of the human mind to imagine
that virginity could be a virtue.

VOLTAIRE

1. How should the word 'clitoris' be pronounced?

    (a) KlitORis?
    (b) KLIToris?
    (c) KLYtoris?

2. Name the famous historic lover whose name translated into English means 'John Newhouse'.

3. Who or what were Titus Perlens, Orchis Extract and Goat Gland?

    (a) Aids to male potency?
    (b) Characters in Oscar Wilde's sexual satire Lady Windermere's Fanny?
    (c) Ingredients used by witches to promote fertility?

4. How is the vagina formed in the male-to-female gender reassignment ('sex change') operation?

5. Which sex act does the *Kama Sutra* say should be reserved for eunuchs, and would certainly not be indulged in by a man of good reputation?

(a) Anal sex?
(b) Oral sex?
(c) Mutual masturbation?

6. In modern usage the word 'glamorous' describes a voluptuous and beautiful woman, but what was the original meaning of 'a glamour'?

7. A 'dolmen' is a megalithic structure consisting of a large stone resting on top of two upright stones. What does it symbolise?

8. Patagonian Indian men use a *guesquel* to give their women intense orgasms. What is a *guesquel*?

(a) A furry leaf from the plant Cortaderia (pampas grass)?
(b) The penile bone of a walrus?
(c) A penis ring made from coarse mule hair?

9. How did the phrase 'in the buff' originate as a euphemism for naked?

10. A 1973 study ungallantly divided women into two groups – sexually attractive or sexually unattractive – and then asked them which risqué seaside postcards they preferred. Which group preferred postcards showing attractive women being desired by men, and which group preferred postcards showing passive men being dominated by women?

On the Game

No nation was ever ruined by trade.

BENJAMIN FRANKLIN

1. Who was Joseph Hooker, who is said to have given his name to the colloquial term for a prostitute?

> (a) An American civil war army general?
> (b) A wealthy 19th-century American pimp?
> (c) A Victorian British anti-vice campaigner?

2. 'Red light' districts are so called because ...

> (a) They show 'blue' films?
> (b) They are no-go areas?
> (c) The colour red has sexual connotations?

3. The English word 'fornication' derives from the Latin word *fornix*. What is the connection?

(a) Fornix means 'arch'. Roman prostitutes used to service their clients beneath the arches of the Coliseum.
(b) Fornix means 'facing north'. The Roman 'red light' district was on the north side of the Tiber.
(c) Fornix means 'furnace'. Vulcan, the Roman god of fire, was also the god of prostitutes.

4. What was an *essayeur* in a Parisian brothel?

(a) A trainee prostitute working a probationary period?
(b) An experienced prostitute employed to try out new clients of uncertain reputation?
(c) A man employed to fondle the prostitutes and so create a conducive atmosphere for the clients?

5. What did the prostitutes of ancient Phoenicia and Egypt wear in order to advertise their skills at oral sex?

6. The Romans defined prostitution as having three characteristics: (1) it was done for money; (2) it was done for the public; and (3) It was done ... how?

> **(a) By women?**
> **(b) For men?**
> **(c) Without pleasure?**

7. Martha Jane Cannary was a 19th-century American frontierswoman whose occupations included that of prostitute. Why was she known as 'Calamity Jane'?

> **(a) Because demand for her services put other prostitutes out of business?**
> **(b) Because she spread venereal disease among her clients?**
> **(c) Because she shot clients who didn't pay promptly?**

8. Ancient cultures practised sacred prostitution, in which temple priestesses acted as sexual intermediaries between worshipper and deity. Where was the oldest recorded temple brothel?

(a) Alexandria?
(b) Babylon?
(c) Sodom and Gomorrah?

9. Name the only American state in which prostitution is legal.

10. What is the average career length of an illegal prostitute in Texas, according to a 20-year study of 1,000 prostitutes?

(a) 2 years?
(b) 5 years?
(c) 10 years?

Sexy Words (2)

Do not say all that you know,
but always know what you say.
CLAUDIUS

What is the meaning of the following words?

1. JACTITATION

(a) Arousal from bragging about sexual exploits.
(b) A scientific term for premature ejaculation.
(c) Breast fondling.

2. MASLUB

(a) A Victorian anti-masturbation device.
(b) Naked Arabian holy nomads who were allowed free sexual favours.
(c) A 1920s sexual lubricant.

3. EUCLUNIUS

(a) Pretty-buttocked.
(b) Flat-chested (of a woman).
(c) Well-hung (of a man).

4. TRIPSOLAGNIA

(a) Drug-induced sexual ecstasy.
(b) The tendency to be sexually aroused by going on a journey.
(c) Sexual arousal from having hair shampooed.

5. CORDAX

(a) A special hemp rope used for bondage.
(b) A lust-inducing ancient Greek dance.
(c) A South American mushroom with supposed aphrodisiac qualities.

6. APISTIA

(a) Impotence.
(b) Unfaithfulness.
(c) Sexual congress with primates.

7. BUMASTOUS

(a) Big-breasted (of a woman).
(b) Well-hung (of a man).
(c) Big-bottomed.

8. QUADOUSHKA

(a) A lesbian Aztec queen.
(b) A slang term for a Russian prostitute.
(c) Sexual teachings of the American Cherokee Indians.

9. ECDEMOLAGNIA

(a) The tendency to be more lustful when away from home.
(b) The ability to achieve orgasm by skin touch alone.
(c) A liking for hairy buttocks.

10. SA

(a) An orgiastic Polynesian fertility festival.
(b) The invisible semen of the Egyptian sun god Ra.
(c) A Tantric sex mantra.

Religious Sex

No man's religion ever survives his morals.

ROBERT SOUTH

1. According to the Bible, an aged King David lay with a Shunammite in order to restore his vigour or 'get heat'. Who or what was a Shunammite?

(a) A virgin girl?
(b) A prostitute?
(c) An adolescent boy?

2. The Christian doctrine of 'original sin' stemmed from Adam and Eve's temptation by Satan in the Garden of Eden and their discovery of the evils of nakedness and sexuality. When was the doctrine of original sin formulated?

(a) Before the lifetime of Jesus?
(b) By Jesus?
(c) After the lifetime of Jesus?

3. Why were Shakers, an American 18th-century offshoot of Quakers, not allowed pets?

4. Early Buddhist monks were governed by numerous rules aimed at avoiding sexual temptation. What was the only circumstance under which a monk was permitted to ejaculate?

(a) After purification?

(b) Between the hours of 8am and 9am?

(c) When asleep?

5. What is the connection between the penis and a hot cross bun, the baked bread with a cross on top now traditionally eaten at Easter?

(a) The hot cross bun was originally shaped like a penis?

(b) Eating a bun was supposed to pardon the sin of masturbation?

(c) Yeast was supposed to inhibit masturbatory tendencies?

6. One of the principal pilgrimage sites in India is the Amarantha Cave in Eastern Kashmir, where believers come to see the 3m-tall (10ft-tall) penis of the god Shiva. Of what is the phallic formation made?

(a) Ice?

(b) Rock?

(c) Salt?

7. Under Catholic law, what must a prospective pope have?

(a) A record of at least five years' celibacy?
(b) Intact genitals?
(c) Healthy sperm?

8. What does the Jewish religious observance *niddah* forbid?

9. What was the first religion to celebrate sexuality?

(a) Hinduism (India)?
(b) Shinto (Japan)?
(c) Taoism (China)?

10. According to the Bible, Eve tempted Adam with an apple. True or false?

Sex on Film

Sex is more exciting on the screen ...
than between the sheets.
ANDY WARHOL

Name the following films.

1. A 1992 film in which Sharon Stone captivates a roomful of men by uncrossing her legs and revealing that she has forgotten to put on any underwear.

2. A 1968 film in which Mia Farrow is impregnated by the Devil.

3. A 1971 film that traces the sexual adventures of two men played by Jack Nicholson and Art Garfunkel.

4. A 1993 film in which Robert Redford offers Woody Harrelson a million dollars to sleep for one night with his wife, played by Demi Moore.

5. A 1972 film in which Woody Allen plays a sperm.

6. A 1976 film in which a 12-year-old Jodie Foster plays a New York child prostitute.

7. A 1978 film in which a 12-year-old Brooke Shields plays a New Orleans child prostitute.

8. A 1994 film in which Demi Moore sexually harasses Michael Douglas in the office.

9. A 1993 film in which Madonna, accused of using rough sex to murder her wealthy lover, drips hot wax on to her lawyer, played by Willem Dafoe.

10. A controversial 1973 film famous for its 'pass the butter' anal sex scene between Marlon Brando and Maria Schneider.

31

Like and Unlike (2)

All women become like their mothers.
That is their tragedy. No man does. That's his.
OSCAR WILDE

What do the four items in each of the following questions have in common?

1. Hot rod
   Joystick
   Swashbuckler
   Torpedo

2. Niggle
   Serd
   Swink
   Swive

3. The Fitting on of the Sock
   Pounding on the Spot
   The Rainbow Arch
   The Tail of the Ostrich

4. Ampallang
   Apadravya
   Dydo
   Guiche

5. Attila the Hun
   Pope Leo VIII
   President Felix Faure of France
   Nelson Rockefeller

Which of the four items in each of the following questions is different from the others and why?

6. Cunnilingus
   Fellatio
   Irrumation
   Penosugia

7. Bugaboos (Canada)
   Mamores (Scotland)
   Paps of Anu (Ireland)
   Tetons (USA)
   Clue: toponymy

8. Justine
   The 120 days of Sodom
   The Story of O Philosophy in the Bedroom
   Clue: Sadism

9. In and Yo (Japan)
   Osir and Neph (Egypt)
   Shiva and Shakti (India)
   Yang and Yin (China)

10. Grandfather
    Grandmother
    Nephew
    Niece
    Clue: playing at home

32

Artistic Sex

The same forces which go to fertilise
a woman and create a human being
go to create a work of art.
FRÉDÉRIC CHOPIN

1. What is unusual about the genitals of the famous marble statue of David by the Italian sculptor Buonarroti Michelangelo (1475–1564)?

2. Name the 20th-century Spanish surrealist whose paintings include *The Great Masturbator* (1929) and *Young Virgin Autosodomised by her own Chastity* (1954).

3. Name the 20th-century Spanish surrealist and cubist who in later life concentrated on intimate drawings of the female genitals.

4. Name the French sculptor whose work includes many bold and realistic portrayals of the female genitals. One of his most famous works is the 1886 marble statue entitled *Le Baiser* ('The Kiss').

5. According to Greek and Roman mythology, Venus was born out of the foam of the sea. In his masterwork *The Birth of Venus*, which depicts this event, why does Italian Renaissance painter Sandro Botticelli (1445–1510) have her rise from the sea in a scallop shell?

6. Many early artistic portrayals of mythological deities are *ithyphallic*. What does this mean?

7. Name the French Impressionist painter whose work *Olympia* (1865) outraged Parisian society by depicting a naked woman reclining on a bed and staring unashamedly at the viewer.

8. Name the Italian Renaissance painter whose anatomical sketches of dissected human cadavers did much to clarify the workings of the sexual musculature.

9. Ancient Hindu erotic art often depicted Indian princes copulating with one or more women while *simultaneously*, among other things, drinking tea, shooting guns and sitting on an elephant. What was the point of all this action?

10. Why was French Impressionist painter Toulouse-Lautrec (1864–1901) called 'Teapot' by the girls in the brothel where he lived?

33

Pot Pourri (5)

Do not suppress your feelings,
choose whatever you will,
and do whatever you desire …
Perfection can be attained
by satisfying all one's desires.
GUHYASAMAJA TANTRA

1. What is a heterosexist?

2. Who is the patron saint of virgins?

> **(a) St Nicholas?**
> **(b) St Valentine?**
> **(c) St Virginus?**

3. What is the origin of the term 'scarlet woman', formerly used as a euphemism to describe a promiscuous woman?

> **(a) The colour scarlet was traditionally associated with brothels?**
> **(b) The term comes from the Old French escarlate, meaning 'promiscuous'?**
> **(c) The term was used by Saint John in the Bible?**

4. What is unusual about the erect phallus of the Giant of Cerne Abbas, a 1st-century BC earth sculpture cut into an English hillside?

5. The word 'pornography' comes form ancient Greece. What did it originally mean?

(a) Sexually explicit material?
(b) Material written by prostitutes?
(c) Written material banned by the Senate?

6. Bioenergetics is a branch of psychotherapy that distinguishes between climax and orgasm. According to bioenergetics, a climax is characterised by contractions of the genital muscles. What contractions characterise an orgasm?

7. What are Ben-wa balls?

(a) Metal balls inserted into the vagina for sexual stimulation?
(b) A slang term for religious orgies held annually in the Ben-wa district of Thailand?
(c) A painful affliction of the testicles?

8. The term 'tribadism' is used as a synonym for lesbianism, but it is also used to describe a sex act that is available only to lesbians. Describe it.

9. How many calories does each partner burn during an average sex act?

> **(a) 50 calories?**
> **(b) 100 calories?**
> **(c) 200 calories?**

10. Would you recommend this book to your friends?

Answers

1

Round the World Sex

1. (c) One hundred million.

2. Vatican City, a state that has been independent of Italy since 1929.

3. All three! Semen was also rubbed on wounds, given to babies as a strengthening drink and used as an all-purpose cure-all and pick-me-up.

4. (c) France. The nearest mile-high mountain to Britain is Crête de Neige (5,653ft/1,723m) in the Jura mountains.

5. The *kagura* is a sacred striptease in which a dancing priestess exposes her genitals to the assembled crowd. In the *tokudashi* a woman encourages the audience to study her vulva with the aid of magnifying glasses and torches. Both rituals celebrate the power of the female genitals.

6. (b) Italy. The elected deputy was Ilona Staller, known as Cicciolina.

7. The Venus Temple is a sex museum that contains a variety of sexual artefacts, such as a Marilyn Monroe mannequin whose skirt blows up when you push a button.

8. (b) Kuwait. The country's Islamic Law Committee also forbids kissing in public, among other subversive practices.

9. The handkerchief has been held under the man's armpit, which secretes pheromones that have an aphrodisiac effect.

10. (c) Germany in 1962. The first sex shop in the world was opened by Beate Rotermund, widow of a Luftwaffe pilot, in the town of Flensburg. The firm Beate Ushe now employs hundreds of people.

Answers

2

Men's Bits

1. (b) 17.

2. The penis is more sensitive to touch after an erection. This can be shown by touching the surface with the two points of a hairpin and measuring how far apart they need to be before they can be felt as two points rather than one. Before erection they need to be 5–9mm apart; during erection they need to be 9–15mm apart; after erection they need to be only 3–4mm apart (the same as on the tip of the clitoris, which is exceeded in sensitivity only by the tip of the tongue).

3. (c) 28 miles per hour (except where speed restrictions apply).

4. (c) 200,000,000 to 400,000,000. No wonder men find sex tiring.

5. The dartos and cremaster muscles relax and contract to raise and lower the testicles in the scrotal sac, thereby ensuring that they are always kept at the correct temperature, which is slightly cooler than the rest of the body.

6. (b) 75%. Only 17% dress to the right and the rest don't seem to mind.

7. Nature has arranged for one testicle to hang lower than the other so that they don't get crushed against each other. In right-handed men the left-hand testicle usually hangs lower (and may be slightly larger), and vice versa in left-handed men.

8. (b) 4 to 5. Nocturnal erections occur during REM (rapid eye movement) sleep and are not necessarily related to sexual dreams.

9. The prostate is an organ that secretes a jet of white alkaline fluid in which sperm is propelled out of the penis. This fluid accounts for about half the volume of semen and protects sperm from the acidic environment of the urethra and vagina.

10. (a) 30 calories, making oral sex an attractive meal-time alternative for weightwatchers as part of a calorie-controlled diet.

Answers

Famous Lovers

1. He made her shave off her pubic hair. In countries where sex began at an early age, bald genitals had erotic connotations.

2. Queen Cleopatra of Egypt (c.68–30BC). Her two lovers were Julius Caesar and Mark Antony. Shaw wrote *Caesar and Cleopatra* and Shakespeare wrote *Antony and Cleopatra*.

3. Lady Emma Hamilton.

4. Abélard and Héloïse. Pierre Abélard (1079–1142) lectured at Notre Dame Cathedral, where he fell in love with Héloïse (1101–1164), the niece of the Canon. Their bodies were reburied in the same grave in 1817.

5. Grigory Aleksandrovich Potemkin (1739–91). Eisenstein's renowned film was called *Battleship Potemkin*.

6. Lancelot and Guinevere. The king was Arthur, legendary King of the Knights of the Round Table, of whom Sir Lancelot was one.

7. Troilus and Cressida.

8. Locks of pubic hair.

9. Romeo and Juliet, made famous by Shakespeare's 1596 play.

10. Adam and Eve.

Answers

True or False (1)

1. True. A man's penis is much bigger than a gorilla's, even though the gorilla's body is three times as bulky. The only purpose of such a large penis would appear to be for female pleasure.

2. False, but at the court of James I girls went about bare-breasted as a sign of virginity.

3. True. According to a study by Sydney University and the Royal Prince Alfred Hospital, the male hormone testosterone makes the throat 'floppier'. Women and men with low testosterone levels snore less.

4. True.

5. True (allegedly).

6. False. According to an American survey, the reverse is the case – working wives have sex twice as often as housewives.

7. False. Nitroglycerine forces blood to rush to the penis and causes an instant erection (*nb* handle with care).

8. True. Alaskan Inuit (Eskimo) women neither menstruate nor ovulate during the winter, and men's sperm count decreases. Research points to absence of light as the cause.

9. False.

10. False. Cold water boosts production of sex hormones in both men and women. Studies of infertility treatment show that cold baths can double a man's sperm count in two to three weeks.

Answers

Musical Sex

1. 'Let's Spend the Night Together'. The lyrics were changed to 'Let's spend some time together'.

2. 'Love to Love You Baby'.

3. Rod Stewart. The song was 'D'Ya Think I'm Sexy?'

4. *Unfinished Music No. 1: Two Virgins*.

5. 10CC (an overestimate).

6. Jim Morrison of the Doors.

7. *This Is Spinal Tap*.

8. Sexual healing. The song was called '(Sexual) Healing' in the UK and 'Sexual Healing' in the US.

9. George Michael. The song was 'I Want Your Sex'.

10. The track is called 'Sexy Sadie'.

Answers

6

Sexual Myths

1. In pagan times the phallic maypole represented an erect penis whose worship would fertilise the earth and ensure good crops. The dance round it added a female element. Until early Christian times the dance ended with a free-for-all orgy in the fields.

2. Sneezing. The connection between semen and nasal mucus is perpetuated by nasophiles, for whom nose blowing is a simulation of ejaculation.

3. (b) As a method of conception. Rain, which fertilised the soil of 'mother' earth, was often viewed as divine semen.

4. The gingerbread man was a cookie that was usually baked by a witch for a woman who wished to cast a love spell over a man. While the witch did the baking, the naked woman, sometimes with the aid of a male assistant, reached orgasm. Later, the woman delivered the gingerbread man to the man of her choice.

5. Spontaneous generation. This doctrine was supported by the Church to explain why the Garden of Eden was a paradise for Adam and Eve – only later did horrible things like flies and insects come spontaneously into being. Not until Louis Pasteur discovered micro-organisms in the 19th century did the doctrine of spontaneous generation die out.

6. According to 12th-century historian Eustathius, the Amazons believed that deprivation of one extremity would be compensated for by increased vigour in the genital extremity, making their captives better lovers.

7. (b) A hermaphrodite.

8. According to mistaken prevailing medical opinion, supported by Church views on the sinfulness of any sexual act that was not for the purpose of procreation, loss of male and female sexual fluids, especially semen, diminished vital energy to the point of madness and death.

9. The Aristotelian view was that a woman's body played no part in conception but acted merely as a passive carrier for the new life created by the man. The Hippocratic view supported the 'two semen' theory, which contended that conception arose from an intermingling of male semen with vaginal secretions.

10. (a) Evil spirits that molested people while asleep. The Succubus was a female spirit that attacked men and drained them of their vital energy, causing nocturnal emissions. The Incubus was a male spirit that seduced or raped women while they slept. Witches were burned for consorting with these spirits.

Answers

7

Pot Pourri (1)

1. The male equivalent of nymphomania is 'satyriasis', named after the part-human, part-goat satyrs of Greek mythology, who had an insatiable sex drive. A generic term for both nymphomania and satyriasis is 'erotomania'.

2. (a) Couples aged 18–24 (average 12 times per month). Couples aged 25–34 have sex an average of 8–11 times per month; couples aged 35–44 have sex an average of 8 or less times per month; and couples aged over 45 have sex an average of 4 times per month.

3. The perineum is called a 'taint' because iT AIN'T one thing or the other.

4. Both indulge in group sex. A bigynist is a man who indulges with two women, whereas a bivirist is a woman who indulges with two men.

5. During sexual intercourse the nasal tissues swell, causing a blocked or runny nose, known in folklore as 'honeymoon nose'.

6. Mistletoe is traditionally associated with magical power and sexual potency. The custom of kissing under the mistletoe at Christmas is a watered-down version of the orgies that took place during the Roman winter fertility festival of Saturnalia. From this custom arose the superstition that a girl who was not kissed under the mistletoe would remain infertile. It was common practice for the early Christian Church to take over pagan festivals such as Saturnalia and substitute its own (Christmas).

7. (b) Corn Flakes. Dr John Harvey Kellogg was a misguided but zealous believer in the dangers of masturbation, which he held responsible for everything from acne to insanity. Believing that the practice was encouraged by spicy food, he invented Corn Flakes as an anti-masturbation cereal. Sugar was added by Kellogg's successors to increase sales.

8. A heart.

9. Grigori Rasputin (1871–1916).

10. The popular explanation of why the letter X is used to represent a kiss is that it looks like two mouths kissing, but the custom is more likely to derive from the practice in illiterate medieval times of signing a document with a letter X, then kissing it to signify sincerity.

Answers

Fashionable Sex

1. A bustle. In the 18th century, 'bustle' was a euphemism for posterior.

2. In French a 'brassière' is a baby's vest (UK) or undershirt (US). The French word for what the English refer to as a 'bra' is *soutien-gorge*, which literally means 'throat support'.

3. (a) The Crusaders. Evidence points to the introduction of chastity belts from the Middle East in the Middle Ages, but another influence may have been Homer's *Odyssey*, in which Hephaestos, the Greek god of metal-working, forged a chastity device for his errant wife Aphrodite.

4. The codpiece – a glove-like appendage that often exaggerated the size of the wearer's own appendage. In France the codpiece was called a *braguette*, which today means (trouser) 'fly' and may have given us the word 'brag'.

5. The kangaroo corset was an S-shaped corset that accentuated the bust and bottom of its wearer.

6. A boy was dressed in feminine attire in order to embarrass him if he got out of hand. Such attire might include short pants or a kilt worn with girl's underwear or no underwear, with lots of soft fabrics, frills and bows.

7. (b) 1965. It was sold in her King's Road boutique and became a symbol of Swinging London.

8. A garter, warm from the bride's leg.

9. (a) A merkin is a female pubic wig used, for example, to cover missing hair or to change hair colour. In the 17th century the word was used as a euphemism for the female genitals.

10. Frederick's of Hollywood is a museum of lingerie worn by film stars.

Answers

9

Sexy Words (1)

1. (a) Deep-bosomed.

2. (c) Sexual application of stinging nettles.

3. (b) The German word for scrotum.

4. (c) Easily penetrated.

5. (a) A pimp's wages in Chaucerian times.

6. (a) Sexual arousal from tickling.

7. (b) Naked medieval Balkan Christian heretics who advocated free sex.

8. (c) The desire of a woman to expose herself to a doctor.

9. (a) An Egyptian fertility god.

10. (c) Lust-provoking.

Answers

10

Aphrodisiacs

167

1. (b) Ginseng. Although prized for its health-giving properties, its aphrodisiac reputation derives historically from its human shape.

2. 'Spanish fly' or 'cantharides'. The active ingredient cantharidin has several damaging effects, including a urethral inflammation that induces a false erection.

3. They reduced it to powder and drank it in water.

4. (a) Oyster. He would eat 50 for breakfast. The historical use of the oyster as an aphrodisiac was based on its suggestive appearance and succulence, but it is also a rich natural source of zinc, which is important for both male and female fertility and of which there are high concentrations in the prostate and semen.

5. The tomato. In 17th-century England the tomato's suggestive colour and texture were too much for Cromwell's puritans, who attempted to eradicate the fruit by spreading scare stories that it was poisonous.

6. Musk. Musk deer are a small variety of deer native to Asia. In some countries musk is used in food for its supposed aphrodisiac qualities. Experiments show that the scent of musk is the smell most easily detected by women. Because of its price, it is often synthesised for use in perfumery.

7. (c) Rhinoceros horn. In the east the horn is ingested in powdered form. Apart from its phallic shape, it contains a urethral irritant similar to Spanish fly.

8. Chocolate. It was brought to Europe from South America by the conquistadors, but because of its aphrodisiac qualities it was banned from use by the Inquisition. Regrettably, if you eat enough chocolate for it to have any amatory effect, you will be too sick to do anything about it.

9. The truffle. Its supposed aphrodisiac qualities derive from the fact that it emits an odour chemically similar to the pheromone that male pigs emit to attract females.

10. They are both anaphrodisiacs or anti-aphrodisiacs, which means that they act to lower the sex drive. Caffeine is a nervous stimulant that can cause anxiety, while nicotine is a nervous depressant that can lead to erection/lubrication problems. In ancient Greece, coffee and tobacco were unknown; women saving themselves for an orgy would eat garlic to keep men away.

Answers

11

Women's Bits

1. (b) About 8–10cm (3–4in), but it stretches to accommodate a penis or a baby.

2. The G spot was named after German obstetrician and gynaecologist Ernst Gräfenburg, the first modern physician to describe it (in 1950). It is a sensitive spot in the front wall of the vagina, about 2in from the entrance. In many women, deep pressure on the G spot is highly arousing and leads to orgasm. The nature and very existence of the G spot continues to arouse scientific debate.

3. (a) Before/at menstruation 74%; (b) around ovulation 14%; (d) after menstruation 7%; (c) at/after menstruation 5%. The figures represent the percentage of women who say they are keenest on sex at that time, according to Shere Hite's *The Hite Report* (1976).

4. *Amatripsis* is masturbation by rubbing the labia together.

5. (b) The existence of female ejaculation has been scientifically proven. Fluid that is not urine is ejaculated by some women. Whether this fluid comes from the urethra, the vagina or glands such as Skene's Glands at the vaginal entrance still arouses scientific debate.

6. Yes. Breasts consist mainly of fat cells and glandular tissue, but there are small muscles that control nipple erection.

7. (c) 10cm (4in). The clitoris has a tip, a body and two legs. The sensitive, pea-like tip, about 0.6cm (¼in) long, is the only part that is visible, at the front junction of the labia minora. The body, about 1.8cm (¾in) long, is concealed by the clitoral hood. The internal legs continue for another 7.5cm (3in) down each inner thigh.

8. Freud considered a woman frigid if she did not achieve a vaginal orgasm, through stimulation of the vagina, rather than a clitoral orgasm, through stimulation of the clitoris. Sex researchers Masters and Johnson overturned this view by stating that all orgasms involved clitoral stimulation, but

then Gräfenburg discovered the G spot within the vagina. Current views tend towards an orgasmic continuum rather than two distinct types, and Freud's view should be confined to history.

9. The fourchette is the point where the labia minora join together at the back, just in front of the perineum. Fourchette is the French word for 'fork'.

10. (a) The ballooning of the inner vagina. During orgasm the uterus lifts up and causes the inner vagina to expand, while the entrance to the vagina becomes tighter and grips the penis. Sex researchers Whipple and Perry later noted that this applies mainly to a clitoris-based orgasm. During orgasm involving G spot stimulation and ejaculation they noted instead an 'A-Frame effect', in which the upper part of the vagina compresses and pushes the penis out.

Answers

12

Historical Sex

1. Valentine's Day commemorates the martyrdom of St Valentine, who was stoned to death in 269. The day was previously celebrated as Lupercalia, the Roman festival of youth – a day for romance and courtship games. It was common practice for the early Christian Church to take over pagan festivals and substitute its own, even if, as in this case, the match was a poor one: St Valentine was renowned for his chastity.

2. (c) 90%.

3. Spectators bet on which woman would reach orgasm first from saddle gyration.

4. (b) 1670s. Dutch doctor Regnier de Graaf (1641–73) was the first to see an ovum under a microscope and recognise its importance in reproduction. Independently, but around the same time, master microscope-maker Anton van Leeuwenhoek (1632–1723) was the first to see and name spermatozoa.

5. A dildo. Olive oil was applied to it before use.

6. (b) One third.

7. The 19th-century equivalent of having sex on a plane was having sex on a train.

8. (a) 1928.

9. The French term 'libertin' originally meant 'free-thinker' and was first used to describe 17th- and 18th-century intellectuals who rejected the strictures of the Church in favour of free enquiry in the pursuit of knowledge. Its immoral connotations arose because the Church accused libertins of debauchery in order to discredit them. Eventually they came to indulge in the licentious behaviour of which they were accused, but whether this was a conscious reply to the Church's stance is unknown. The word libertin derives from Liber, the Roman god of wine and sexual ecstasy.

10. (b) A sewing machine. The article was called 'The Influence of Sewing Machines on Female Health' and expressed concern about the possibility of sexual arousal caused by the constant motion of the foot treadle.

Answers

13

Pot Pourri (2)

1. The gonads. If the gonads are testicles the person is male, if the gonads are ovaries the person is female, regardless of the appearance of the person's outward genital organs.

2. (b) 1953. At its peak in the early 1970s it sold 7 million copies a month.

3. (b) Kinsey used something similar to cotton buds/Q tips.

4. Gilbert and Sullivan. Unlike their more famous comic operas, *The Sod's Opera* was never publicly performed.

5. According to legend, Peeping Tom peeped at Lady Godiva (*c*.1040–80), wife of Leofric, Earl of Mercia. Leofric rashly promised to reduce taxes if his wife rode naked through the streets of Coventry. Everyone stayed indoors but Tom took a peek and was struck blind for his effrontery.

6. (a) An erection restraint similar to a large bicycle clip.

7. Pheromones enter the nose, but instead of

triggering the olfactory system they are directed straight to the hypothalamus in the brain.

8. She was a 'striptease artist'. Mencken equated her removal of feathers with moulting.

9. A virgin was originally any girl or woman who was not bound to any man. It was in this sense that goddesses such as the Greek Artemis (Roman Diana), goddess of the hunt, were 'virgin goddesses'. Only when patriarchal marriage became the norm and husbands demanded an 'untouched' bride did virginity begin to assume its modern meaning. In many old languages the word for 'virgin' and 'maiden' was the same, which caused all sorts of misunderstandings about 'virgin births' for later religions.

10. (c) Waking up (10%); (a) heavy exertion such as jogging (4%); (b) sexual intercourse (1%). The figures refer to the percentage of heart attacks caused by each activity, according to a study by the Harvard Medical School.

Answers

14

Censorship

1. The animated film *Snow White and the Seven Dwarfs*. The sexual possibilities of Snow White, seven dwarfs and a bed were too much for the censors.

2. Under a local 19th-century law pre-dating the advent of cinema, the film was considered to be obscene because it depicted topless (native) girls.

3. *The Pawnbroker*.

4. (b) *Lady Chatterley's Lover* by D. H. Lawrence.

5. Pussy Galore in *Goldfinger* (1964). United Artists were about to change her name to Kitty Galore until producer Cubby Broccoli convinced the American censors that what was good enough for Prince Philip was good enough for the American public.

6. Her original name was Titty.

7. Bowdlerisation. The *Family Shakespeare* (1818) was published by Dr Thomas Bowdler (although it was his sister Henrietta who did the expurgating).

8. (a) 3 seconds. Other rules restricted marital sleeping arrangements (couples had to sleep in separate beds) and physical contact (both parties had to keep at least one foot on the floor).

9. *Henry and June*, which was about the relationship between Henry Miller, his wife June and Anaïs Nin.

10. To prevent piano legs arousing men because of their resemblance to women's legs, they were covered with baggy linen (the piano legs, that is, not the men).

Answers

15

Marital Sex

1. The custom of carrying the bride over the threshold derives from the practice of bride capture, in which men kidnapped and carried away brides from other tribes. Bride capture was practised in England until the 15th century, in Ireland until the 18th century and in parts of South America until recently.

2. (a) 16%. Of that 16%, less than one third completely disapproved of premarital and extramarital sexual relations.

3. Nubile originally meant simply 'ready or suitable for marriage'. The word comes from the Latin *nubere*, meaning 'to marry'.

4. The sight of his wife's pubic hair.

5. (b) 6,156. The ceremony was conducted by Reverend Sun Myung Moon, head of the Unification Church.

6. Virginal blood was supposed to have devilish properties that could make a less powerful man impotent.

7. They are both forms of polygamy, in which there is more than one wife or husband. In polygyny a man has two or more wives simultaneously, in polyandry a woman has two or more husbands simultaneously. When there are two or more husbands and wives, the term used is 'group marriage'. In Tibet, for example, whole groups of brothers traditionally married whole groups of sisters.

8. (a) Denmark.

9. The custom of kissing the bride is a watered-down version of the old practice of bridal prostitution, in which the bride was expected to have sex with wedding guests before her husband. The practice stemmed from the ancient fear of the blood of a deflowered bride (see Answer 6).

10. Among Brahman men, brothers had to marry in age sequence, the eldest first. To free a younger brother to marry, an elder brother could go through a mock wedding in which he married a tree.

Answers

16

Like and Unlike (1)

1. They are all condoms, available in various countries.

2. They all claimed or are said to have had more than 1,000 lovers.

3. They are all types of incest. Fratrilagnia is incest with a brother, Patrilagnia is incest with a father, Sororilagnia is incest with a sister and Thygatria is a general term for father/daughter incest.

4. They are all sexual positions in the *Kama Sutra*.

5. They were all celibates.

6. They are all descriptions of a same-sex preference, but homosexuality is unlike the other three because it applies to both male and female. Cymbalism, lesbianism and sapphism all describe female homosexuality only.

7. They are all slang for testicles, but marbles is unlike the other three because it is not *rhyming* slang: 'cobblers' *awls*', 'Niagara *Falls*', 'orchestra *stalls*'.

8. They are all types of vagina in the *Kama Sutra*, except Tiger. The Deer has a capacity of six finger widths, the Mare nine finger widths and the Elephant twelve finger widths. According to the *Kama Sutra*, it is possible to tell the type from a woman's outward appearance.

9. They are all books by Henry Miller, except Hexus.

10. They are all colloquial terms for sexual liaisons, but fling is unlike the other three because it is not restricted to a short, specific time of the day. A *Cinq à sept* takes place in the early evening, a 'matinee' takes place in the afternoon and what happens at a 'flunch' requires little stretch of the imagination.

Answers

Sexual
Technique

1. The embryonic Church adopted the patriarchal pre-Christian teaching of the Stoics, which allowed sexual intercourse only in the man-on-top position. This teaching was later propagated by Catholic missionaries to the South Pacific, where local women named the position and ridiculed its passivity.

2. The woman 'milks' the man's penis by abdominal and vaginal muscle contractions. Unfortunately for men, the technique requires extensive training, and modern woman thinks she has more constructive ways of spending her time.

3. *A posteriori* sexual intercourse enables the penis to apply friction to the front wall of the vagina, where the G spot is located. The position also facilitates manual manipulation of the clitoris.

4. The butterfly flick is a fellatio technique. The woman flicks her tongue lightly along the underside of the penis. Experts can do it without having to use hands to steady the object of their attentions.

5. The refractory period is the period following orgasm during which further sexual response does not occur. It occurs in nearly all men and lasts from a few minutes to a few hours; in women it is much less common and may not occur at all, making multiple orgasm possible.

6. Kegel exercises (or pelvic floor exercises) were developed for women by gynaecologist Dr Alfred Kegel in the 1940s. They consist of a series of exercises designed to strengthen the pubococcygeus (or PC) muscles that surround the vagina. Weak PC muscles, common among Western women, can lead to lack of vaginal sensitivity, urinary stress incontinence and other problems. Healthy PC muscles that can be used to grip the penis intensify sexual pleasure for both partners. Healthy PC muscles are also necessary for *kabazzahs* (see Question 2) and belly dancers, and they also facilitate childbirth; Eastern 'showgirls' use their PC muscles to propel ping pong balls across a room. Women can become familiar with their PC muscles by practising contracting, holding and relaxing them, e.g. to stop and start the flow of urine. It sometimes helps to insert a finger or other

instrument into the vagina to give it something to grip. Kegel exercises for men give firmer erections and greater ejaculatory control.

7. The man lies down, legs apart, knees raised. The woman crouches on him between his legs, facing away from him.

8. The lips and tongue.

9. *Karezza* ('caress') is a technique in which both partners refrain from orgasm and ejaculation during sexual intercourse. Its aim is to prolong erotic play. The term was coined by Dr Alice Bunker Stockham in 1883, but the technique was practised long before by Taoists, who believed that the quantity of a man's semen was limited and had to be preserved. The Catholic Church opposes the technique because it involves sexual intercourse not intended for conception.

10. (b) Music, (a) alcohol, (c) perfume or body odour, (d) sex talk. Further down the list of preferred sex accompaniments or preliminaries were (in order) drugs, pornography and food.

Answers

18

Royal Sex

1. Princess Anne, who won a gold medal as a member of the British equestrian team.

2. (a) They had to go without beer for a month.

3. It is said that in the 1885 Act of Parliament that made male homosexuality a criminal offence, legislation against lesbians was abandoned because Queen Victoria could not imagine how they did it. Similar legislation was also abandoned in 1921 on the grounds that drawing attention to the practice of lesbianism might encourage it.

4. (b) Marie Antoinette (1755–93), Queen of France and wife of Louis XVI.

5. The Egyptian royal family based succession to the throne on matrilineal ties (i.e. to the mother rather than the father), because paternity could never be proved. Therefore the only way for a son to rule was if he married his sister. Ptolemy was married to his sister Cleopatra when he was 10 and she was 14.

6. (b) Three. She also had six fingers.

7. The pubic hairs of his mistresses.

8. (c) Fourteen. Only Claudius was heterosexual.

9. Sarah Ferguson, Duchess of Kent. Podophilia is an attraction to or fetish for feet. While estranged from her husband Prince Andrew, Ms Ferguson was photographed clandestinely having her toes sucked by another man.

10. (b) By performing cunnilingus on her. Paintings depict the empress standing open-robed while her visitors kneel before her and pay their respects.

Answers

19

Sexy
Anagrams

1. Heterosexual.

2. Sexual intercourse.

3. Simultaneous orgasm.

4. Ejaculation.

5. Multiple orgasms.

6. Y chromosome.

7. Nymphomaniac.

8. Prostitution.

9. Masturbation.

10. Contraceptive pill.

Answers

20

Pot Pourri (3)

1 Eros was the Greek god of love. His Roman counterpart was Cupid.

2. (c) By shaving her head.

3. Castration complex. Some feminists have suggested that what Freud regarded as envy of the penis was no more than simple interest in the penis.

4 (a) An Arab strap is a ring that fits round the base of the penis to maintain an erection.

5. The urethra is extended by means of a catheter, which is then covered with skin from the abdomen to form the penis body.

6. (c) For each suitor she throws a pip on the fire. If the pip makes no noise then the associated suitor is not truly in love with her, but if the pip pops then he too is bursting with love for her.

7. The Nobel Sperm Bank is a repository for the sperm of Nobel Prize winners, for use in artificial insemination. It was founded in 1980 in Escondido, California.

8. (a) Petting.

9. The horseshoe is a symbol of the vulva. The superstition stems from ancient times when worship of the female sex organs was widespread.

10. (d) Being made love to by an imaginary lover (56%); (b) being overpowered and forced to surrender (49%); (a) satisfying more than one man (43%); (c) acting as a prostitute (25%). The figures represent the percentage of women reporting these fantasies, according to a 1974 New York study. (d) is the most common fantasy reported. The only other fantasy reported by more than 50% of women is reliving a previous sexual experience.

Answers

21

Literary Sex

1. *Memoirs of Fanny Hill*.

2. The *Kama Sutra* ('Love Text'). The book is concerned mainly with skills useful in finding and supporting a spouse, such as household skills for women and gambling for men. Only its central section discusses sexual practices. The 12th-century *Koka Shastra* and the 16th-century *Ananga Ranga* are more sexually detailed and complete.

3. *The Perfumed Garden (for the Soul's Delectation)*. Among other things, the book lists 35 types of penis and 38 types of vagina. Its section on homosexuality is usually omitted from English translations.

4. Sir Richard Burton (1821–90). He was knighted in 1887 for his multi-volume translation of *The Thousand and One Nights*, also called *The Arabian Nights*.

5. Anaïs Nin (1903–77).

6. *Moll Flanders*. The extraordinary complete title of the novel is *The Fortunes and Misfortunes of the Famous Moll Flanders, &c.*

who was Born at Newgate, and during a Life of continued Variety for Threescore Years, besides her Childhood, was Twelve Year a Whore, five time a Wife (whereof once to her own Brother), Twelve Year a Thief, Eight Year a Transported Felon in Virginia, at last grew rich, liv'd Honest, and died a Penitent. Written from her own Memorandums.

7. Hans Christian Andersen (1805–75), author of fairytales such as *The Ugly Duckling*, *The Emperor's New Clothes* and *The Snow Queen*.

8. Masturbation – a common Victorian explanation for ailments of all kinds.

9. *Pygmalion*. The original Pygmalion was a Greek sculptor who fell in love with one of his statues, whom the goddess Aphrodite brought to life at his request. Agalmatophilia is a fetish for statues.

10. Jane Austen (1775–1817). The novel is *Emma*.

Answers

22

True or False (2)

1. True. While growing up they elongate their penis by dangling rocks from it. (Hence the proverb: a man with a knot in his penis should beware an erection.)

2. False. The sex of the reproductive organs is *determined* at the time of fertilisation but it is not until the male hormone testosterone is released that the clitoris grows to form a penis and the testicles descend to become differentiated from ovaries. These external differences do not become apparent until about the seventh or eighth week.

3. False.

4. True. There is no scientific evidence for any connection between male/female genitals and outward appearance.

5. True. New Guinea tribes did try to halt the spread of venereal disease by holding orgies, with disastrous consequences. Ritual orgies were a common method of appeasing gods and resolving problems.

6. True. He called the boys his 'minnows'.

7. False. *Cassoulet* is a stew originating from France. The odour secreted by a woman's body is called *cassolette*.

8. False. Homosexual behaviour has been observed in numerous species.

9. True. The Latin word *testis* means 'witness'. The gesture of holding the testicles was equivalent to the witness saying, 'castrate me if I lie'. With the advent of Christianity the practice died out.

10. False. Historical note: the British doctor who conducted Napoleon's autopsy commented on the smallness of the penis and cut it off for a souvenir, which has changed hands a number of times since.

Answers

23

Animal Sex

1. None. All mammals have the same size sperm; only the shape differs.

2. The kangaroo's penis hangs behind the scrotum.

3. The vagina of a female octopus is in her head. More specifically, it is the same tube through which she breathes.

4. Male deer masturbate by gently rubbing their antlers against a tree or through vegetation. The whole process takes about ten seconds. As with the penis, antler growth and sensitivity is regulated by hormonal secretions from the testicles.

5. The female threadworms stick their vaginas out of the skin of the vegetables and the males crawl around the surface in search of them.

6. (c) The whale.

7. Like the human female, the female gibbon is not subject to an oestrus cycle, which restricts sexual receptivity to the period

around ovulation. This means that she can be receptive to the male at all times, which encourages pair-bonding because the male requires no other partner to satisfy his sexual needs.

8. The greater the number of sexual liaisons in which the female ape indulges, the greater the number of males willing to protect her young, because the young might belong to them.

9. A motile penis moves in and out of its own accord during mating, requiring no effort on the part of its owner. The human male can only view with envy the evolutionary luck of elephants and bats.

10. The female cat cries out because the penis of the tomcat has backward-pointing barbs. It is the vaginal stimulation provided by these barbs that brings about the release of eggs for fertilisation.

Answers

24

Contraception

1. A half-lemon was inserted into the vagina like a diaphragm. As well as being a barrier to sperm, its acidity acted as a spermicide. Casanova was a well-known lemon advocate.

2. (a) Camels. Arab camel drivers discovered that inserting a stone into a female camel's uterus prevented the camel from becoming fertile during long desert crossings. How they discovered this is not known.

3. The original purpose of the condom was to protect the wearer from syphilis. The term 'prophylactic', which is sometimes used as a synonym for condom, means 'protecting from disease'. Casanova was a well-known condom advocate.

4. (a) Animal bladder. Sheep gut was the most common condom material, but the intestines of other animals and materials such as fish skin were also used. The modern condom did not appear until after the invention of vulcanised rubber in the 1840s.

5. 'Durex' is an acronym of DUrable, Reliable, EXcellent.

6. (c) 1930. The Catholic Church approved the rhythm method following physiological and hormonal research in the 1920s that led to breakthroughs in the understanding of the menstrual cycle.

7. Dung. It may have been used compacted as a cervical plug, or in more viscous form to soak up or reduce the mobility of sperm. On the other hand, perhaps the process of applying it was enough to deter potential suitors.

8. (b) The Bellonese did not understand the idea of contraception because they did not understand the mechanics of conception. They believed that children were sent by ancestral deities and that sexual intercourse was purely for pleasure. The missionaries soon taught them otherwise.

9. (a) Condom, in south-west France.

10. Sexual abstinence – the only 100% effective contraceptive method.

Answers

25

Unconventional Sex

1. An autopederast can insert his penis into his own anus.

2. (b) Stretch their labia minora. The Hottentot apron or *mfuli* was the name given to the elongated labia minora of African tribes such as the Baganda and the Bagishu. Stretching was achieved by pulling or by tying the labia together with string and dangling a rock from them. The genital modification was highly prized by the men, but for everyday tasks the labia, often several inches long, were tucked out of the way into the vagina.

3. Biting (not necessarily involving the breaking of the skin). In The Line of Jewels biting is done by all the teeth (as opposed to The Point, where only two teeth are used). The Broken Cloud is a 'bite' applied to the breast, in which the skin is raised into the spaces between the teeth.

4. (a) Removal of pubic hair by pulling it out in clusters.

5. An axillist puts his penis in his partner's armpit. A shaven armpit is said to be more

arousing than a hairy armpit, but designer stubble can be painful.

6. (a) Flagellation. The practice of flagellation for sexual arousal has a long history but became more prevalent in Victorian Britain after caning became a common form of school punishment.

7. Masochism is named after Leopold von Sacher-Masoch. De Sade (1740–1814) and Sacher-Masoch (1835–95) were novelists who wrote respectively about practices involving the inflicting and receiving of pain for sexual pleasure. Their names were later used to describe such practices.

8. A Prince Albert is a metal ring that is inserted lengthways through the tip of the penis. Prince Albert is said to have worn one to keep his foreskin retracted for cleanliness. Victorian men used them to tie their penis down while wearing fashionably tight trousers. As a sexual stimulant a Prince Albert gives firmer pressure for both partners during sexual intercourse.

9. (c) *Coitus à cheval* originally referred literally to sexual intercourse on a horse. The rocking gait of the horse provided impetus and rhythm to penetration.

10. *Tsutsumi* is the ancient Japanese art of packaging the penis to offer as a gift to the lover. Intricate designs concocted with silk and ribbons made unwrapping arousing for both partners.

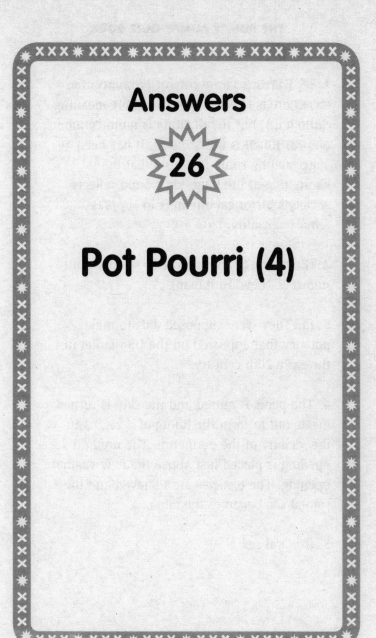

Answers

26

Pot Pourri (4)

1. (c) KLYtoris is the correct pronunciation based on its Greek origin (probably meaning 'little hill'), but (b) KLIToris is more common and (a) KlitORis is also used. It has been suggested by some feminists that the shortening of the long 'kly' sound reflects society's historical attempts to suppress female sexuality.

2. Giovanni Casanova (*casa* = 'house' and *nuova* = 'new' in Italian).

3. (a) They were supposed aids to male potency that appeared on the US market in the early 20th century.

4. The penis is gutted and the skin is turned inside out to form the lining of a vagina in the vicinity of the perineum. The urethral opening is placed just above the new vaginal opening. The testicles are removed and the scrotal sac becomes the labia.

5. (b) Oral sex.

6. 'A glamour' was originally a magic spell that witches were said to cast on a man to cause him to imagine that he had lost his penis. The testimony of men afflicted by such hysteria caused women to suffer horrible deaths as witches. In Scotland 'glamour' became a synonym for 'grammar' because the occult was associated with learning.

7. A 'dolmen' symbolises the vulva or gateway to the womb. At the Crucuno dolmen in France during the autumn equinox, sunlight is channelled into the form of a pubic triangle. In olden times women would lie on dolmens to increase their fertility.

8. (c) A penis ring made from coarse mule hair. It fits on the end of the penis with the hairs pointing downwards.

9. 'Buff' is an adjective that describes undyed leather or animal skins. 'Buff skin' was an early term for deer hide, and to go 'in stag' or 'in buff' became 16th-century slang for going unclothed, with just one's skin.

10. The attractive women preferred postcards showing passive men being dominated by women, while the unattractive women preferred postcards showing attractive women being desired by men.

Answers

27

On the Game

1. (a) General Joseph 'Fightin' Joe' Hooker (1814–79) was an American general. The use of his name as a colloquial term for prostitute may derive from his penchant for prostitutes during the California Gold Rush or from the women that followed his brigade during the Civil War.

2. (c) The colour red has sexual connotations. In ancient China it was associated with womanhood and sexual power. Later, 'wine houses' that provided brothel services advertised by putting bamboo lamps of red silk outside their doors. The custom reached the USA in the 19th century when Chinese flocked to the California Gold Rush. *nb* Experiments show that the colour red speeds up an erection.

3. (a) *Fornix* means 'arch'. Roman prostitutes used to service their clients beneath the arches of the Coliseum.

4. (c) A man employed to fondle the prostitutes and so create a conducive atmosphere for the clients. There are worse jobs.

5. Lipstick. This may have been the original purpose of lipstick, although another explanation of its origin is that it was invented to mimic the sexual arousal of the genital labia.

6. (c) Without pleasure.

7. (b) Her nickname is said to derive from the venereal diseases she spread among her clients.

8. (b) Babylon, c.2000 BC. Every Babylonian woman entered the temple of Ishtar, the goddess of sexuality, at least once in her life in order to become a temporary sacred prostitute. The occupation held no stigma but incensed the Hebrews of the Old Testament, who named the city of Babylon 'the great whore'.

9. Nevada. Prostitution was not technically illegal anywhere in the US until a series of laws outlawed it in the early 20th century. In 1973 the Nevada Supreme Court upheld the right of counties with fewer than 50,000 inhabitants to license brothels, and state-wide there are now 36 legal brothels.

10. (b) 5 years.

Answers

28

Sexy Words (2)

1. (a) Arousal from bragging about sexual exploits.

2. (b) Naked Arabian holy nomads who were allowed free sexual favours.

3. (a) Pretty-buttocked.

4. (c) Sexual arousal from having hair shampooed.

5. (b) A lust-inducing ancient Greek dance.

6. (b) Unfaithfulness.

7. (a) Big-breasted (of a woman).

8. (c) Sexual teachings of the American Cherokee Indians.

9. (a) The tendency to be more lustful when away from home.

10. (b) The invisible semen of the Egyptian sun god Ra.

Answers

29

Religious Sex

1. (a) A Shunammite was a virgin girl. In many cultures it was believed that contact with young girls could revive the ardour of old men. The practice was known as Shunammitism.

2. (c) After the lifetime of Jesus. It was St Paul in the 1st century who, amid religious controversy about when sin first entered the world, linked the first sin with Adam and Eve, but it was the neurotic views of St Augustine (354–430) that set Christianity's future, sex-negative, agenda. 'Between faeces and urine we are born,' he wrote. He linked sin to sex and suggested that sin was propagated from parents to children by sexual reproduction. Hence the necessity for Jesus to be born of a virgin.

3. Shakers were not allowed to have pets because of the possibility of seeing them mate, which might arouse sexual feelings. As in some other religions, sexual energy was sublimated into religious ecstasy, achieved in this case by frenzied dancing or shaking.

4. (c) A Buddhist monk was permitted to ejaculate only when asleep or unconscious. One prurient tale of what was permissible told of a monk who fell asleep by the wayside with an erection that was made use of by a number of passing women.

5. (a) The hot cross bun was originally shaped like a penis. Roman phallic worship died out slowly in the early days of Christianity and, when the Church turned springtime fertility festivals into Easter, worshippers continued to wear phallic amulets and carry bread baked in a phallic shape. The Church compromised by allowing phallic buns to be carried as long as they were marked with a cross. Since that time the shape of the bun has been modified.

6. (a) Ice. The cave contains a stalagmite of ice that has formed in the shape of a phallus.

7. (b) Intact genitals. A castrate or someone with deformed genitals is not allowed to become pope. At one time the pope sat on a special chair that exposed his genitals to a procession of cardinals, who would confirm

their approval by chanting 'testiculos habet et bene pendentes'. The law stemmed from the prevalence of eunuchs in the Church. The hiring of castrati for their singing voices was not stopped until 1878.

8. Niddah forbids sexual intercourse during menstruation. It is one of the world's harshest menstrual taboos, requiring that the husband have no physical contact with his wife ('even with his little finger') for 10–14 days a month. Judaism has many laws that restrict indulgence at designated times. Niddah is an example of man's ancient fear of menstrual blood, whose regular and inexplicable appearance, unassociated with sickness, came to be associated with magic and witchcraft.

9. (c) Taoism (China). Followers of Tao believed that harmony was achieved by the mingling of male and female essences (Yang and Yin), each needing the other. While a woman's Yin essence was inexhaustible, a man's Yang essence was limited but could be strengthened by absorption of Yin essence during sexual intercourse, which was therefore encouraged as much as possible.

Taoists practised intercourse without ejaculation, viewed masturbation as a waste and celibacy as a neurosis.

10. False. The Bible refers only to 'the fruit of the tree which is in the midst of the garden'. In Muslim tradition the fruit was the banana or Indian fig, because Adam and Eve covered themselves with fig leaves. The apple tradition may have come from ancient Greece and Rome, where apples had erotic symbolism and were exchanged by lovers. The tale of an errant female bringing about the downfall of mankind may have been intended to promote patriarchal religion over goddess worship.

Answers

30

Sex on Film

1. *Basic Instinct.*

2. *Rosemary's Baby.*

3. *Carnal Knowledge.*

4. *Indecent Proposal.*

5. *Everything You Always Wanted to Know About Sex (But Were Afraid to Ask).*

6. *Taxi Driver.*

7. *Pretty Baby.*

8. *Disclosure.*

9. *Body of Evidence.*

10. *Last Tango in Paris.*

Answers

Like and
Unlike (2)

1. They are all types of vibrator.

2. They have all at one time been synonyms for having sex. Chaucer referred to 'swinking', but 'sard' is even older. The *Lindisfarne Gospels* of 698 translate, 'Thou shalt not commit adultery' as 'Ne serd the othres mones wif'.

3. They are all sexual positions from *The Perfumed Garden*.

4. They are all rods or rings that are inserted into the male genitals for decoration and for sexual stimulation of male or female. An Ampallang is a metal rod that pierces the tip of the penis from side to side. An Apadravya is a metal rod that pierces the tip of the penis from top to bottom. Dydoes are smaller metal rods that pierce vertically through the rim of the tip. A Guiche is a metal ring that pierces the perineum behind the scrotum.

5. They all died while having sex.

6. They are all synonyms for oral stimulation of the penis, except cunnilingus, which is oral stimulation of the vulva and clitoris.

7. They are all mountain ranges named after breasts (Mam, Pap, Teat), except the Bugaboos of Canada.

8. They are all books by the Marquis de Sade, except *The Story of O*, which was written by Pauline Réage.

9. They are all expressions or representations of the male/female duality in the universe, except Osir and Neph (Egypt). The Egyptian equivalents are Geb (god of the earth) and Nut (goddess of the sky), which is an opposing view to the Judao-Christian concept of a Father in Heaven and a Mother Earth.

10. In the UK it is legal to have sex with a grandmother, nephew or niece, but not a grandfather. Only marrying them is forbidden. It is also legal to have sex with aunts, uncles and cousins, but not with parents, children, siblings, half-siblings or step-children/step-parents.

Answers

32

Artistic Sex

1. David's genitals are too small compared to the rest of his body. This inconsistency may have been the result of artistic modesty or censorship, or it could be that Michelangelo intended to reflect the ancient Greek idea that a small penis was more aesthetically appealing and more potent, because sperm had less distance to travel.

2. Salvador Dali (1904–89).

3. Pablo Picasso (1881–1973).

4. Auguste Rodin (1840–1917).

5. The scallop is an ancient European symbol for the vulva, with its roots in the Norse word *skalpr,* meaning sheath or vagina. Botticelli's scallop is a symbol for the birth of Venus out of the vulva of the sea.

6. They are depicted with an erect phallus (of often exaggerated proportions).

7. Edouard Manet (1832–83).

8. Leonardo da Vinci (1452–1519).

9. The intention was to demonstrate the virility of the subject.

10. The girls called him Teapot because of his physique. Owing to a medical condition he had a hunchback and an oversized penis.

Answers

33

Pot Pourri (5)

1. A heterosexist is someone for whom only heterosexual relationships are acceptable. Someone who is afraid of homosexuals is called a homophobe.

2. (a) St Nicholas.

3. (c) The term comes from a description by St John of an unholy woman in the Bible's Book of Revelation: 'I saw a woman sit upon a scarlet-coloured beast, full of names of blasphemy ...'

4. It is too big. The figure is 60m tall and the phallus is 12m long, reaching up to the chest. In olden days women wishing to become pregnant would sleep on the phallus overnight.

5. (b) Material written by prostitutes.

6. In bioenergetics an orgasm is characterised by contractions that spread through the entire body.

7. (a) Ben-wa balls are two metal balls that are inserted into the vagina to provide sexual stimulation while walking. It is said that hollow centres with mobile weights provide the best results.

8. Tribadism is the rubbing together of pubic mounds for mutual clitoral stimulation.

9. (b) During an average sex act each partner burns only 100 calories, but no one said you have to be average.

10. Yes!